BIRD GUIDE: Land Birds East of the Rockies

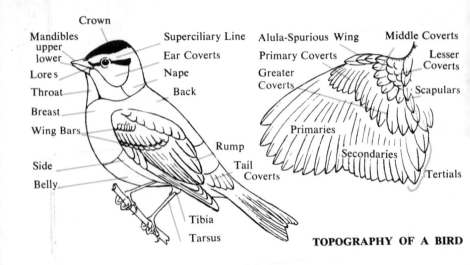

Crown

Mandibles
upper
lower

Lores

Throat

Breast

Wing Bars

Side

Belly

Superciliary Line

Ear Coverts

Nape

Back

Rump

Tail
Coverts

Tibia

Tarsus

Alula-Spurious Wing

Primary Coverts

Greater
Coverts

Primaries

Secondaries

Middle Coverts

Lesser
Coverts

Scapulars

Tertials

TOPOGRAPHY OF A BIRD

SCREECH OWL *Otus asio* 10 inches

These friendly birds, smallest of the "horned" owls, are one of the best-known and most abundant members of their family. They come in two color phases—reddish brown and gray—which have no relation to age, sex, or season. They are found in open woodlands, orchards, and shady cities and suburbs; they have been thought to mate for life and sometimes occupy the same tree for years, often sleeping in the nest cavity during the day. The downy young are nearly white. Screech Owls feed at night, their diet consisting largely of small rodents and insects.

Note: A mournful, wavering trill, often believed to be an omen of death or other misfortune; also a steady trill without change in pitch. **Nest:** Usually in a hole in a tree, though nesting boxes are sometimes used; three to five white eggs, 1.35 x 1.20. **Range:** Resident from southern Canada to the Gulf, Texas, and Mexico.

31 Family Strigidae: True Owls

HORNED OWL *Bubo virginianus* 25 inches

These big, fierce-looking owls are distinguished by the ear tufts and the white throat band. In flight they seem neckless. The general color is dark brown, but subspecies of the North and West may be more grayish and very pale or very dark. Horned Owls are the most savage, most active, and most destructive of their family. They hunt on dark days and at night and are strong enough to kill skunks, woodchucks, rabbits, poultry, and domestic cats. The species is justly unpopular with farmers, but in the wilderness it is useful in preserving the balance of nature. Other foods include insects, snakes, and small owls.

Note: A series of *hoo's,* somewhat like those of the Barred Owl but less distinctly accented; a loud, unearthly shriek. **Nest:** Usually the deserted nest of a hawk, heron, or crow; also in caves and hollow trees; two or three white eggs, 2.25 x 1.85, are laid in February or March. **Range:** Resident from Labrador and Alaska to South America.

Family Strigidae: True Owls   32

SNOWY OWL *Nyctea scandiaca* 25 inches

No ear tufts. Plumage white, more or less heavily marked with grayish or black, the female usually being quite strongly barred on the back. These owls are locally abundant in the Far North, where they prefer the low tundra to the more heavily timbered districts. They hunt by day from lookouts not far aboveground and feed upon hares, lemmings, ptarmigan, ducks, and fish which they catch in the shallow water among rockweed-covered stones. Cyclic flights, presumably because of food shortages on the tundra, bring them far down into the United States during the winter about once every four years.

Voice: A hoarse, ravenlike croak; a whistling cry.
Nest: On the ground in dry spots on the tundra; often a natural depression is lined with moss and feathers; two to eight smooth white eggs, 2.25 x 1.75. **Range:** Breeds throughout the Arctic tundra. The southward flights (see above) seldom bring them below the northern United States.

33 Family Strigidae: True Owls

HAWK OWL *Surnia ulula* 15 inches

This owl is well named. Its barred under parts, its long tail, its hawklike sitting posture and flight, and its habit of feeding by day rather than at night make it seem more like a hawk than an owl. In hunting it skims about close to the ground, pausing at intervals to rest on a lookout perch from which it may make swift descent upon its prey. It feeds on lemmings and other small rodents, but it also takes larger game such as hares and ptarmigan, and insects also are important in the diet.

Voice: A hawklike chatter, a whistle, and a screech have been reported. **Nest:** In cavities in old dead trees or stumps, occasionally in the deserted nests of other birds; four to eight white eggs, 1.60 x 1.27. **Range:** Breeds in spruce and pine forests of northern Canada; winters in southern Canada and northern United States, appearing very rarely as far south as New Jersey and Ohio.

Family Strigidae: True Owls 34

BURROWING OWL *Speotyto cunicularia* 10 inches

Legs very long and scantily feathered; barred tail short and stubby; no ear tufts. These little brown owls are abundant in the prairie regions west of the Mississippi, where they are always seen on or near the ground. They live in burrows which they sometimes dig themselves but usually appropriate from prairie dogs or other animals. They hunt by day as well as night, and during the day are often observed sitting in or near the burrow entrance. Food consists chiefly of night-flying insects and small rodents.

Note: A sharp alarm; a *coo* similar to that of a Mourning Dove; another call reminiscent of that of a Yellow-billed Cuckoo. **Nest:** At the end of a burrow, five to ten feet deep, one to three feet underground; six to ten white eggs, 1.25 x 1.00. **Range:** West of the Mississippi Valley north to southern Manitoba and British Columbia, south to Florida and the West Indies.

BARRED OWL *Strix varia* 20 inches

A big gray-brown owl without ear tufts; eyes dark brown; tail short; breast crossbarred, belly streaked up and down. Throughout its range this is usually the most abundant of the large owls. Its call might be mistaken for that of the Horned Owl, but should not be, for this species is much less savage and destructive than the other. Barred Owls are quite noisy and from late afternoon until early morning may cry out to one another across a stretch of woodland. They respond readily to crude imitations of their call and frequently come close to investigate. Their home base is generally in deep woodland, but they range widely, feeding on mice and other small rodents, insects, frogs, and small birds.

Note: Eight hoots, grouped in twos—*hoohoo-hoohoo-hoohoo-hooah*—are characteristic. **Nest:** Usually in hollow trees in deep woods; two to three white eggs, 1.95 x 1.65. **Range:** Resident in eastern North America from Newfoundland south to Florida and the Gulf Coast.

Family Strigidae: True Owls 36

GREAT GRAY OWL *Strix nebulosa* 27 inches

This large owl is found in the United States only in the northern states in winter. Its tail is unusually long, and its feathers are so long and loose that it appears to be much bigger than is actually the case. It is without ear tufts, the facial disks are very large, and the small eyes are yellow. It is dark gray above, mottled with white, and has heavy vertical streaks of brown on the under parts. It feeds mostly in the evening and subsists largely on mice and hares.

Note: Hoots and a cry similar to that of a Screech Owl. **Nest:** Of sticks and twigs, lined with leaves and moss, usually in dense evergreens; two to five white eggs, 2.15 x 1.70. **Range:** Breeds from Hudson Bay and Alaska southward to the northwestern United States; winters south to the northern border of the United States, casually appearing farther south when the normal food supply fails.

37 Family Strigidae: True Owls

LONG-EARED OWL *Asio otus* 15 inches

This species derives its name from its unusually long ear tufts, which are quite narrow and set close together. The face is buff or brown, the under parts white and buff with streaks of brownish black.

This owl is often quite common, but its presence is not easily detected. It usually spends the day sitting upright in a dense evergreen, and when it ventures forth at night to feed, its voice is not heard so often as that of some other owls. Crows sometimes discover it during the day and proclaim its whereabouts with their incessant cawings.

Voice: A rather quiet bird which gives low moans and whines when disturbed near its nest. **Nest:** Uusually the abandoned nest of a crow or squirrel, usually in an evergreen tree; four to seven pure white eggs, 1.55 x 1.23. **Range:** Breeds from coast to coast and from Newfoundland and Ontario south to Virginia, Tennessee, and Texas; winters from southern Canada to the Gulf.

Family Strigidae: True Owls 38

SHORT-EARED OWL *Asio flammeus* 16 inches

Ear tufts so short as to be seldom visible; general color, buffy, paler than most owls; breast distinctly streaked; tail barred.

Frequenting grasslands and marsh, this owl hunts by night and day, "hawking" close to the ground, often scooping up a field mouse or other prey without pause. Sometimes it watches from a post or stump until a victim comes into view and sometimes it watches at a mousehole like a cat. Often several of the birds are observed feeding over the same area.

Voice: Mostly silent, except around the nest, where hisses and cluckings are emitted; during the mating season a series of *toots* uttered close together. **Nest:** Usually on the ground, in marshes, fields, or prairies; four to seven pure white eggs, 1.53 x 1.22. **Range:** Breeds from the Arctic regions south to New Jersey and Kansas; winters from Massachusetts and southern Ontario to Florida and the Gulf.

39   Family Strigidae: True Owls

TENGMALM'S OWL *Aegolius funereus* (ABOVE)   10 inches

About the size of a Screech Owl, but without ear tufts; dark brown above, spotted with white; grayish white below, striped with brown. These birds of the northern coniferous forests are rare and irregular winter visitors to the United States, seldom penetrating very far below the border. They can sometimes be picked up by hand.

SAW-WHET OWL *Aegolius acadicus* (BELOW)
7½ inches

Similar to above, but smaller and much commoner in the United States; bill black instead of yellowish, as with Tengmalm's Owl; no ear tufts. Nocturnal and shy, the presence of this bird is most readily revealed in late winter and early spring, when its varied calls (including one that sounds like saw filing) are heard in the dense woodlands which it frequents. Breeds from northern United States northward.

Family Strigidae: True Owls   40

CHUCK-WILL'S-WIDOW *Caprimulgus carolinensis*   12 inches

Male with white ends on outer tail feathers and narrow band of buffy white across the lower throat, both of which the female lacks. The birds are generally brown and gray, so speckled and streaked with black as to be almost invisible as they sleep through the day perched lengthwise on a limb or concealed on the ground near a stump or rock. All goatsuckers have very small bills and very large mouths, suitable for catching night-flying insects. Their plumage is soft, their flight noiseless. They feed near the ground, usually at dusk or in the early morning.

Note: A loudly whistled and often repeated *chuck-will's-widow* with the accent on the first syllable. **Nest:** None; two creamy white eggs, 1.40 x 1.00, blotched with brown and lavender, laid on bare ground or dead leaves. **Range:** South Atlantic and Gulf states, breeding north to Virginia, west to Texas; winters southward to northern South America.

41   Family Caprimulgidae: Goatsuckers

WHIP-POOR-WILL *Caprimulgus vociferus* 9¾ inches

In appearance much like the Chuck-will's-Widow; the male has broad white tail patches. This bird is often confounded with the Common Nighthawk, but can readily be distinguished by the lack of white wing patches, the shorter wings, the rounded tail, and, close at hand, by the long bristles around the bill. Whip-poor-wills are more nocturnal than nighthawks and on moonlight nights may continue the whistled repetition of their name nearly all night long. Like other members of the family, they feed on flying insects.

Note: An emphatically whistled *whip-poor-will* with the accent on the first and last syllables, sometimes endlessly repeated. **Nest:** None; two grayish or creamy white eggs, 1.15 x .85, mottled with pale brown, gray, and lilac, are deposited on the ground in the woods. **Range:** Eastern North America, breeding from the Gulf to southern Canada and westward in the southern part of its range to Arizona; winters in southern states and southward.

Family Caprimulgidae: Goatsuckers   42

POOR-WILL *Phalaenoptilus nuttallii* (ABOVE)   7½ inches

This beautiful little night-jar looks very much like a small whip-poor-will but is grayer and the white tail spots are not so pronounced. It is best distinguished by its mournful night call, *poor-will-ee*, with the accent on the second syllable and the final syllable very weak. Poor-wills are found from the Plains to the Pacific but are not common east of the Rockies.

PAURAQUE *Nyctidromus albicollis*   (BELOW)
13 inches

The female is smaller than the male, and her "white" markings, which are smaller than her mate's, are apt to be buffy. Two eggs, 1.17 x .88, with brown blotches over a salmon-colored base, are laid on the bare ground. The birds are common in the Lower Rio Grande Valley in Texas and southward in tropical America.

43   Family Caprimulgidae: Goatsuckers

COMMON NIGHTHAWK *Chordeiles minor* 10 inches

The white wing patch, which looks like a hole in the wing when the bird is flying overhead, is a good field mark. The male has a white throat and a white band across the tail; the female has a rusty throat and lacks the white tail band. The wings are long and pointed. The birds fly by day as well as night, but are most active at dusk and before sunrise. They frequent open fields and rocky pastures, but they are also common in towns and cities where they are often observed in the late afternoon flying over buildings in pursuit of insects. They eat nothing else, and all their food is caught on the wing.

Sound: A loud, nasal *peent,* usually uttered on the wing; in courtship the male, rising from a deep, swift dive, makes a booming noise with the wings. **Nest:** None; two mottled gray-and-white eggs are laid on the ground or on the gravel roofs of buildings. **Range:** From coast to coast; in eastern North America breeds from Florida to Newfoundland; winters in South America.

Family Caprimulgidae: Goatsuckers, et cetera 44

CHIMNEY SWIFT *Chaetura pelagica* 5½ inches

A smoke-colored, swallowlike bird with narrow wings, which appears tailless as it flies swiftly and erratically through the air in search of small insects. The wings seem to move alternately, though it has been proved with motion pictures that they beat together. The short tail has spiny tips at the ends of the feathers which enable the birds to cling to upright walls and hitch their way along.

Sound: A continuous and not unmusical twittering, uttered on the wing, also within the depths of chimneys, where, combined with the fluttering of the wings, it may be very startling to the householder. **Nest:** A shallow cup of small twigs glued to one another and to the sides of a chimney or hollow tree by the bird's saliva; three to five white eggs, .75 x .50. **Range:** North America east of the plains, breeding from Florida to Labrador; winters in South America.

45 Family Apodidae: Swifts

RUBY-THROATED HUMMINGBIRD *Archilochus colubris* 3½ inches

In certain lights the red throat of the male appears black. The female has a white throat and white tips to the outer tail feathers. Owners of flower gardens have the best opportunity to observe these winged jewels as they whir from blossom to blossom in search of tiny insects and nectar. They can be confused with no other bird, but the big hawk moths, which are about the same size, are sometimes taken for hummingbirds. Hummingbirds are excitable and belligerent and, with their bullet-swift flight and needle-sharp bills, are able to put much larger birds to rout.

Sound: Angry-seeming twitters and squeaks; in flight the rapidly vibrating wings make a humming sound. **Nest:** An exquisite lichen-covered cup, fashioned of delicate plant materials; saddled on the branch of a tree; two white eggs, .50 x .35. **Range:** Breeds from Nova Scotia south to the Gulf; winters from Florida and southern Louisiana southward.

Family Trochilidae: Hummingbirds 46

BELTED KINGFISHER *Megaceryle alcyon* 13 inches

The breast and sides of the male are blue gray like the back. The female has chestnut-colored sides and a chestnut-colored breast band in addition to the blue-gray one. Both have ragged crests.

These kingfishers may be found about ponds, lakes, rivers, or at the seaside—anywhere that small fish may be obtained. They catch their prey by diving from perches on dead branches or by hovering over the water before making the plunge.

Note: A very loud, harsh rattle, easily heard half a mile away on a clear, quiet day. **Nest:** An enlarged chamber at the end of a three-to-five-foot burrow, excavated by the birds in a sandbank which is usually near water; five to eight glossy white eggs, 1.35 x 1.05. **Range:** Breeds from Labrador and Alaska south to Florida and southern California; winters from New Jersey and Ohio southward.

47   Family Alcedinidae: Kingfishers

GREEN KINGFISHER *Chloroceryle americana* 8 inches

Smallest of United States kingfishers; bronzy green above, spotted with white; white below (female buffy), spotted on sides and flanks with blackish green; ragged crown, but no crest. The male has a rufous breast band; that of the female consists entirely of blackish spots. Like the Belted Kingfisher, these birds have three toes in front, one behind, with the middle and outer toes united so as to make the foot an efficient shovel for digging out the nesting burrows. Green Kingfishers catch fish, usually watching for their prey from a sand bar or rock in midstream, but they also feed away from water, where they subsist on insects, lizards, et cetera.

Note: A rattle similar to the Belted's, but shriller and weaker. **Nest:** In a chamber at the end of a horizontal burrow, two to three feet deep, excavated by the birds in a sandbank; four to six glossy white eggs, .96 x .76. **Range:** Southwestern border of United States, from southern Texas and Arizona southward.

Family Alcedinidae: Kingfishers 48

YELLOW-SHAFTED FLICKER *Colaptes auratus* 13 inches

The best field marks are the brown back and, in flight, the conspicuous white rump patch. The underlinings of the wings and tail are golden yellow. Both sexes have a black crescent on the breast, a red crescent on the nape, and the male has black mustache marks. These birds are common in woods and orchards, in shady suburbs, and along roadsides. They do much of their feeding on the ground. They eat ants more than anything else, but they also take other insects and a variety of wild berries and fruit.

Voice: A rapidly repeated *wicker-wicker-wicker* and many other calls and whistles; loud and persistent drumming with its bill against hollow limbs, tin roofs, etc. **Nest:** A cavity in a tree at almost any distance from the ground; five to ten white eggs, 1.06 x .81. **Range:** North America east of the Rockies. Northernmost birds move southward for the winter, traveling in loose flocks.

RED-SHAFTED FLICKER *Colaptes cafer* 13 inches

The linings of the wings and tail in this species are salmon red instead of golden yellow as with the Yellow-shafted Flicker, and the mustache marks of the male are red instead of black. The red crescent is usually lacking on the nape but is sometimes present in individuals. Red-shafted and Yellow-shafted Flickers interbreed in the overlap of their ranges and there are innumerable variations in their markings. Birds have been reported with one side of the mustache red, the other black. The two species are practically identical in habit.

Voice: Similar to that of the Yellow-shafted Flicker. **Nest:** Undistinguishable from that of the Yellow-shafted Flicker. **Range:** Breeds along the Pacific Coast from southeast Alaska to southern Mexico, east to South Dakota, Nebraska, Kansas, and eastern Texas; northernmost birds retire southward in winter.

Family Picidae: Woodpeckers 50

PILEATED WOODPECKER *Dryocopus pileatus* 17 inches

Both sexes have bright red crests, but the forehead of the female is black. The male has red streaks extending back from the bill. The only bird with which this species could possibly be confused is the extremely rare Ivory-billed Woodpecker, which is much larger and has a different pattern of red, black, and white. Pileateds live in deep woods and are so silent that their presence is most often revealed by the squarish or rectangular holes which they drill in trees for ants, grubs, and beetles.

Sound: Similar to the common *wicker* of the flickers, but louder and deeper. Resonant drumming with the bill on hollow limbs during the mating season. **Nest:** Chip-lined cavity in a tree, usually in dense woodland; four to six white eggs, 1.30 x 1.00. **Range:** from southeastern Canada south to Florida, west to Texas. Not found in Rockies but appears again on the Pacific Coast.

RED-BELLIED WOODPECKER *Centurus carolinus* 10 inches

Look for the black-and-white zebra-striped back and the red head (crown of female gray). The reddish tint on the center belly is usually very faint. Common in woodlands of the Southeast, these noisy birds are also found on farms and in cities where trees remain. Besides drilling for the regular woodpecker fare of ants, beetles, and grubs, they also take acorns and fruit, sometimes causing damage to the citrus crop by boring into oranges for juice.

Sound: A sharp, resonant *cha-cha-cha,* repeated; a shrill rattle like a tree frog; various other flickerlike calls. Drumming with the bill. **Nest:** In a hole in a dead tree, usually excavated by the birds, though the abandoned nests of other woodpeckers are sometimes used; four to five white eggs, 1.00 x .75. **Range:** Permanent resident from Delaware to the Gulf Coast and west to Texas.

Family Picidae: Woodpeckers 52

RED-HEADED WOODPECKER *Melanerpes erythrocephalus* 9 inches

Adults with entire head and upper breast bright red; young have grayish-brown heads streaked with darker color. The bold white wing patches are present in all plumages. These handsome birds are the ruffians of the family, very noisy and quarrelsome, especially in the nesting season. Like other woodpeckers, they bore in dead wood for grubs, et cetera, but they also take insects from the air by "flycatching." Much of their food consists of small fruits and berries, and they thrive on acorns and beechnuts in winter.

Sound: A loud, whining *charr-charr;* many other calls, most of which are harsh and unpleasant. Drumming and rapping with the bill. **Nest:** In a hole in a tree, fence post, or telegraph pole; four to six white eggs, 1.00 x .75. **Range:** United States from the plains eastward, breeding from Florida and Texas north to southern Ontario and Michigan. Northernmost birds move southward in winter.

YELLOW-BELLIED SAPSUCKER *Sphyrapicus varius* 8½ inches

Under parts pale yellowish brown. Male with scarlet crown and throat; female with scarlet crown and white throat; young with head and neck mottled gray and white with a few scarlet feathers. In all plumages the longitudinal white wing patch is distinctive. This species has gained ill repute from its habit of boring a circle of holes around a tree trunk, thus at times killing the tree. It feeds both on the sap and on the insects attracted thereby, but its damage is seldom serious. It is a skilled flycatcher and also eats fruit.

Sound: Loud whining *whee* and other harsh calls similar to those of a Blue Jay. Loud irregular drumming with the bill on a hollow tree or resonant limb. **Nest:** In a hole excavated in a tree; four to seven white eggs, .85 x .60. **Range:** From coast to coast; east of the Rockies breeds from Virginia and Missouri to Hudson Bay, wintering in southern United States and southward.

Family Picidae: Woodpeckers 54

HAIRY WOODPECKER *Dendrocopos villosus* 9 inches

In summer these robin-sized woodpeckers are found in heavy woods, where they breed, but in winter they are often seen on trees about houses, hunting in bark crevices for insect larvae. They are extremely valuable birds in the forest because of the borers and bark beetles they destroy. In appearance they are very like the Downy Woodpecker but can always be distinguished by their much larger size (two to three inches) and their proportionately much larger bill. The male has a red patch on the back of the head; the female is all black and white.

Sound: A sharp whistled *peenk;* a rapid series of notes slurred into an unmusical rattle; typical woodpecker drumming against tree trunks and limbs. **Nest:** In holes in living or dead trees, usually in deep woods; three to six glossy white eggs, .94 x .72. **Range:** In one form or another the Hairy Woodpecker is a resident in all forested areas of the United States and southern Canada.

55 Family Picidae: Woodpeckers

DOWNY WOODPECKER *Dendrocopos pubescens* 6 inches

Very similar to the Hairy Woodpecker, but smaller and the bill is not so heavy. The male has a red patch on the back of the neck which the female lacks. Downies are one of the commonest of our woodpeckers, found in orchards, open woods, towns, and suburbs. They are usually very tame, allowing close approach before flying. In winter they come to feeding stations with nuthatches and chickadees if suet is provided. They drill holes in trees similar to those of sapsuckers, but observation has proved them less harmful. In winter especially they destroy many noxious insects, grubs, and larvae, including those of the codling moth and cankerworm.

Sound: A sharp *pik* similar to the Hairy's *peenk,* delivered singly or in rapid series. Typical woodpecker drumming with the bill. **Nest:** A hole in the dead branch or trunk of a tree; four to six white eggs, .75 x .60. **Range:** Southern Canada and Alaska south to the Gulf Coast, Florida, and southern California.

Family Picidae: Woodpeckers 56

RED-COCKADED WOODPECKER *Dendrocopos borealis* (ABOVE) 8¼ inches

Black-capped birds with crossbarring of white on the back. Male with small patch of scarlet on both sides of the head; female without. In actions and habits similar to the Downy, but the voice is harsher and more nasal. The birds frequent open pinewoods in the southeastern United States, west to Texas, and north to Virginia.

LADDER-BACKED WOODPECKER *Dendrocopos scalaris* (BELOW) 7¼ inches

The crown of the male is red, that of the female black; under parts are brownish white. Quite similar to the Downy. It generally nests in trees but also finds fence posts and telegraph poles suitable; four to five white eggs are laid in the nest cavity. The birds are found from Texas to southeastern California and north to Colorado.

BLACK-BACKED THREE-TOED WOODPECKER *Picoides arcticus* (ABOVE) 9½ inches

Back solid glossy black; female's cap black, male's yellow; wings barred with white, flanks with black. Only three toes, two in front and one behind. Breeding in the northern coniferous forest, this species appears more commonly in the United States than the next.

BOREAL THREE-TOED WOODPECKER
Picoides tridactylus (BELOW) 9 inches

Back barred with white; yellow crown patch on male mixed with white. A circumpolar species which usually appears in the United States only in winter. **Voice:** a shrill, loud, nasal shriek, sometimes repeated—similar to that of the above. **Nest:** In a hole in a living or dead tree, also similar to that of Black-backed; four white eggs, .95 x .70. **Range:** The birds breed in northern coniferous forests north to the limit of trees and are circumpolar in distribution.

Family Picidae: Woodpeckers 58

IVORY-BILLED WOODPECKER *Campephilus principalis* 20 inches

Largest and rarest of our woodpeckers; sexes similar except that the crest of the female is black, that of the male red. Note carefully the white pattern on the black body and wings (see Pileated Woodpecker, p. 51). The bill of this species is ivory white, that of the Pileated slate color. The birds are big and powerful and often scale the bark off the greater portion of a tree in search of grubs. They require a large area for feeding, and the cutting off of the great swamp and river-bottom forests of the South is probably the chief reason for their decline. Only a few isolated specimens survive.

Sound: Shrill two-syllabled note with a nuthatch tone; loud rappings on trees with the bill. **Nest:** Hole in a large tree, living or dead, in an impenetrable swamp; three white eggs, 1.45 x 1.00. **Range:** Formerly the South Atlantic states west to Texas and Oklahoma. It is hoped that specimens survive in the great swamps of Louisiana, Georgia, Florida, and South Carolina.

59 Family Picidae: Woodpeckers

EASTERN KINGBIRD *Tyrannus tyrannus* 8½ inches

Dark slate above, white below. The best field mark is the white band at the end of the tail. The orange crown patch is seldom visible.

These noisy, quarrelsome birds—"tyrant flycatchers" indeed—are often observed sitting on wires, posts, or other perches in the open, watching for insects which they catch on the wing. When food is more abundant on the ground, they feed there and at times they take fruit. They are intolerant of other birds and have a special aversion to crows and hawks, which they drive off by dashing down upon them from above and pecking them, often following them for a great distance.

Voice: A series of shrill, harsh sounds; a *thsee-thsee* call is common. **Nest:** Of sticks, rootlets, grass, string, et cetera; placed in trees, in orchards or open woodlands; four or five creamy white eggs, .95 x .70, mottled and streaked with brown and lilac. **Range:** Breeds from the Gulf to southern Canada; winters in tropics.

Family Tyrannidae: Flycatchers 60

GRAY KINGBIRD *Tyrannus dominicensis* 9 inches

Another "tyrant flycatcher," similar to the common Eastern Kingbird but larger and with a much larger bill; paler gray above and without the white band at the end of the tail. The tail is notched, not rounded. The orange-red crown patch is seldom visible. This species is noisy and pugnacious, especially in defending its home territory, but after mating, the birds quarrel, very little among themselves and often several use the same lookout perch from which to dash out after passing flies or moths.

Note: A rapidly repeated, shrill shriek: *pe-che-ri, pe-che-ri,* with the accent on the second syllable. **Nest:** Similar to that of the Eastern Kingbird but more shabbily built; placed in thickets, most often of mangrove trees; three to five pinkish-white eggs, 1.00 x .72, profusely blotched with brown. **Range:** Breeds in West Indies, Florida, Georgia, and South Carolina; winters in the West Indies and Central America.

WESTERN KINGBIRD   *Tyrannus verticalis*   9 inches

The white outer tail feathers are the best field mark.

These "tyrant flycatchers" which are abundant west of the Mississippi are, if possible, even more noisy and pugnacious than the eastern species. They seem always to be trying to find a neighbor to quarrel with, and their great variety of calls and shrieks are rather unpleasant to the ear. Like other kingbirds, they feed chiefly on insects, most of which they catch on the wing.

Note: A shrill, metallic squeak; low twittering; a harsh, discordant scream and other unmelodic notes. **Nest:** Similar to Eastern Kingbird's, placed in trees and in all sorts of other locations, frequently in eave troughs or above windows; four creamy white eggs, .95 x .65, spotted with brown. **Range:** Western United States, breeding from Texas to Manitoba and west to the Pacific; winters south of United States.

SCISSOR-TAILED FLYCATCHER *Muscivora forficata*   14 inches

This pretty creature, which is often known in the Southwest as the "Texan Bird of Paradise," is the most graceful member of the flycatcher family, if not of the whole order of perching birds. Its long tail, which it opens and shuts as it flies, gives it great maneuverability as it swings through the air in pursuit of insects but makes it very awkward on the ground, where it seldom lights. Habits are similar to the kingbird's.

Note: A shrill *tzip, tzip* and other calls reminiscent of the Eastern Kingbird. **Nest:** Quite large; built of such trash as twigs, grasses, paper, rags, string, et cetera; placed at any height in any kind of bush or tree; four to five creamy white eggs, .90 x .67, spotted with brown. **Range:** Breeds from Texas north to Kansas, west to New Mexico, east to eastern Louisiana; winters south of the United States.

63 Family Tyrannidae: Flycatchers

DERBY FLYCATCHER   *Pitangus sulphuratus*   10½ inches

This big, imposing flycatcher cannot be mistaken for any other bird. Crown patch and under parts are bright yellow; wings and tail are rufous; face black and white. On account of the size of the head and bill, often known as the "Bull-headed Flycatcher." This species has the quarrelsome disposition typical of its family, but its heavy body renders it less active than most of its relatives. It watches for its prey from a conspicuous perch, sallying into the air for large insects or diving into the water for small fish. Fruit also is included in its diet. It is found at stream edges, in open country, and in town.

Voice: Loud, shrill call notes, either spaced or run together. **Nest:** A large structure of twigs and rubbish with the entrance at the side; in trees or thorny bushes; three to five creamy white eggs, 1.15 x .82, specked around the large end with brown. **Range:** Lower Rio Grande Valley southward.

Family Tyrannidae: Flycatchers   64

GREAT CRESTED FLYCATCHER *Myiarchus crinitus* 9 inches

The rufous on the wings and tail, the gray throat and yellow belly are the distinctive marks of this large olive-brown flycatcher. During the mating season the birds are very noisy and quarrelsome, defending a wide territory against others of their kind and chasing off all birds that come too near the nest tree. The lookout perches from which they dash into the air for insects are in the tops of tall trees, and much of their feeding is done in the forest canopy.

Note: A loud, clear whistle with a rising inflection, repeated several times. **Nest:** In holes in dead limbs; of straw, feathers, et cetera, usually with a recently shed snakeskin near the entrance; four to six buffy white eggs, .89 x .68, streaked and blotched with brown. **Range:** Eastern North America, breeding from Florida and the Gulf north to southern Canada. Winters in the far South and southward.

65 Family Tyrannidae: Flycatchers

EASTERN PHOEBE   *Savornis phoebe*   7 inches

These gray, sparrow-sized flycatchers are easy to identify, as they sit on a favorite perch not far above the ground, constantly wagging their tails. Formerly they nested in cavities on rock ledges or on the sides of ravines, but today they are more often found nesting inside and outside man-made structures. Their lavish destruction of insects makes them useful around farms.

Note: An emphatic *phoe-be,* often tiresomely repeated. The *phoe-be* call of the Black-capped Chickadee is much softer and has an entirely different tone. **Nest:** Of mud, grasses, and moss, plastered on a beam in a barn or underneath a bridge or under the eaves of a house; often patched up for use year after year; five white eggs, .75 x .55. **Range:** North America east of the Rockies, breeding from north Georgia to Nova Scotia; winters in southern states. Say's Phoebe (*Sayornis saya*) of the dryer western states is paler, with rusty on its under parts.

Family Tyrannidae: Flycatchers   66

YELLOW-BELLIED FLYCATCHER *Empidonax flaviventris* (BELOW) 5½ inches

Of the four very similar *Empidonax* flycatchers in eastern North America this is the most easily separated in the field by sight; the yellow underparts are the distinctive mark. It nests in swamps and bogs in northeastern United States and Canada; winters in Central America.

ACADIAN FLYCATCHER *Empidonax virescens* (ABOVE) 5½ inches

Greenish above; conspicuous eye ring; two white wing bars; yellowish undersides. A bird of the Southeast, it breeds as far north as New York, but never reaches Acadia, the land of Evangeline. Shady woods near water are its favorite resorts. Here the nests are suspended in crotches in the outer branches of bushes or trees at heights of four to twenty feet aboveground. Eggs, .72 x .54, are creamy with brown spots. Winters are spent in the tropics.

67 Family Tyrannidae: Flycatchers

TRAILL'S FLYCATCHER *Empidonax traillii* (NOT ILLUSTRATED) 6 inches

Somewhat larger than others in the *Empidonax* group; found in swampy pastures and alder thickets and around the edges of ponds and lakes, where they nest in low bushes. The common *way-bee-o* call of the East, with the accent on the middle note, is contracted to two syllables in the Midwest.

LEAST FLYCATCHER *Empidonax minimus*
(ILLUSTRATED) 5¼ inches

The *che-bec* call will lead the observer to this flycatcher which is common in orchards, swamps, and along roadsides. The nests, made of plant fibers and grasses closely felted together, are placed in upright forks on any kind of tree or bush, usually not more than fifteen feet aboveground; eggs creamy white, .65 x .50. **Range:** North America east of Rockies, breeding north to southern Canada.

Family Tyrannidae: Flycatchers 68

EASTERN WOOD PEWEE *Contopus virens* 6½ inches

The pewee can best be distinguished from the Eastern
Phoebe, with which it is often confused, by its plaintive
pee-ah-wee, which is strikingly different from the brusque
call of the latter. Also it has two inconspicuous white
wing bars and it does not wag its tail. Pewees are more
likely to be found in high, dry woods; they choose feeding perches near the tops of trees and as a rule are very
difficult to see.

Note: A clear, plaintive whistle, *pee-ah-wee* or *pee-
wee.* **Nest:** Exquisitely fashioned of plant fibers quilted
together and ornamented with lichens; placed at varying
heights in trees in woodlands, occasionally in orchards;
three creamy white eggs, .80 x .55, specked with brown
at the larger end. **Range:** Breeds in eastern North
America from Florida to southern Canada; winters in
Central America and southward.

69 Family Tyrannidae: Flycatchers

OLIVE-SIDED FLYCATCHER   *Nuttallornis borealis*   7½ inches

Somewhat like the Eastern Wood Pewee, but larger; has a large bill, a white throat, and dark patches at the sides of the breast. The distinctive white tufts on either side of the rump are not always visible. The species favors dead pine swamps and openings in coniferous forests. Like other flycatchers, it sallies forth from lookout perches for its prey; it favors Hymenoptera (ants, bees, and wasps) and is not welcomed where bees are kept.

Note: A loud, clear whistle, *whip-wheeu,* which carries for a long distance and serves as a guide to the bird's location; the first syllable is short, the second drawn out to a plaintive ending. **Nest:** Small for the size of the bird; made of twigs and mosses, firmly anchored to horizontal limbs or forks; three to five creamy or pinkish eggs, .85 x .65, spotted about the large end with brown and lavender. **Range:** In northern coniferous forests from Labrador and Alaska to North Carolina and Lower California; winters in South America.

Family Tyrannidae: Flycatchers   70

VERMILION FLYCATCHER *Pyrocephalus rubinus* 6 inches

Female with tinge of pink, where the male has brilliant vermilion similar to that of male Scarlet Tanager. To those accustomed to the demure plumage of most eastern flycatchers the first sight of this, the most gorgeously feathered of American species, is an experience never to be forgotten. Like the rest of the family, it feeds on flying insects; usually from perches near the ground.

Note: During the mating season a twittering song while poised in the air. **Nest:** Saddled on limbs of trees at comparatively low elevations; composed of small twigs and vegetable fibers woven together and often adorned, like the Eastern Wood Pewee's, with lichens; four creamy buff eggs, .73 x .54, wreathed at the large end with bold spots of brown and lilac. **Range:** Breeds along the Mexican border from Texas to Arizona and Lower California and southward; winters in South America.

71 Family Tyrannidae: Flycatchers

HORNED LARK *Eremophila alpestris* 7¾ inches

The tiny, inconspicuous "horns" consist of narrow black feathers. The black on the head and chest of the male is more intense than on the female, and the male has a black forehead. These larks frequent waste places and barren areas both inland and near the shore and are usually seen on the ground. They walk instead of hopping and are apt to be numerous. Seen from below in flight, the black tail is in sharp contrast with the light under parts. Subspecies, e.g., the Prairie Horned Lark, vary locally in color and size.

Voice: Alarm note and call a whistled *tseet, tseet;* song a low twittering warble. **Nest:** A shallow depression in the ground, sometimes lined with grass, sometimes not; three to five grayish eggs, .85 x .60, profusely specked with brown. **Range:** Almost world-wide in temperate grasslands; breeds in eastern North America from Arctic to North Carolina and Texas; winters southward.

Family Alaudidae: Larks 72

TREE SWALLOW *Iridoprocne bicolor* 6 inches

Male, steely blue or green above; female, duller; both sexes always entirely white below. Young have sooty brownish-gray backs, white under parts.

Except when they are skimming over ponds in search of insects, these swallows are apt to be scouring the air above buildings or fields, flying at higher elevations than the Barn Swallows. In late summer and fall they congregate on trees, marsh reeds, or telephone and power wires, hundreds or even thousands together. They destroy many insects but, unlike most swallows, can live on seeds and berries.

Voice: A typical swallowlike twittering; a short warble. **Nest:** Of grass and straw, lined with feathers; placed in a hollow in a tree near water or wet meadows or in bird boxes; four to six white eggs, .75 x .52. **Range:** Breeds in northern United States north to Newfoundland and Alaska; winters in southern United States and southward.

73 Family Hirundinidae: Swallows

BANK SWALLOW *Riparia riparia* (ABOVE) 5¼ inches

Smallest of United States swallows; distinguished by the conspicuous band across the breast, showing in bold relief against the lighter throat. Found throughout the Northern Hemisphere. In North America they breed from the middle of the United States north to the Arctic, nesting in colonies in holes in sandy banks; four or five white eggs, .70 x .50, are laid in an enlarged chamber at the end of a two-to-three-foot tunnel.

ROUGH-WINGED SWALLOW *Stelgidopteryx ruficollis* (BELOW) 5½ inches

Back brown; throat and breast gray. The outer vane of the outer primary is stiff and bristly, thus giving the species its name. Insectivorous, like all swallows, these birds feed on the wing, usually flying low over land or water. They breed in banks or stone crevices from coast to coast and from the northern states south into Mexico.

Family Hirundinidae: Swallows 74

BARN SWALLOW *Hirundo rustica* 7½ inches

Dark steel blue above; forehead and throat chestnut; under parts buffy; deeply forked tail (the true "swallow-tail") with white marks; female is duller than the male.

These beautiful swallows have nearly deserted the rocky cliff ledges and caverns where they formerly nested and are now most common around farm buildings, the beams and rafters of which they appropriate for nesting sites. As insect destroyers they are welcome little neighbors, and some farmers cut small holes in their barns for the convenience of the birds. Food is caught on the wing.

Note: A continuous rapid twitter. **Nest:** A bowl of mud and grass cemented together with saliva and lined with feathers; plastered against a beam or rafter; four or five white eggs, .80 x .55, spotted with reddish brown. **Range:** Breeds throughout the Northern Hemisphere; in eastern North America from North Carolina and Tennessee to Quebec and Manitoba; winters south of United States.

75 Family Hirundinidae: Swallows

CLIFF SWALLOW *Petrochelidon pyrrhonota* 5½ inches

Dark blue above, easily distinguished from the Barn Swallow by the square tail and light, buffy rump, the pale forehead, and the ruddy throat. In the East these are often known as Eaves Swallows because of their habit of plastering their nests on the outside of barns or other buildings, up under the eaves. In the West they usually resort to cliffs, the faces of which are sometimes covered with thousands of their little mud flasks. Like all swallows, these are very useful as destroyers of harmful insects.

Note: A continuous twitter, uttered on the wing or at rest. **Nest:** A flask- or gourd-shaped structure of mud, lined with straw and feathers; attached to buildings (preferably unpainted) or against the sides of cliffs; four or five whitish eggs, .80 x .55, spotted with reddish brown. **Range:** Breeds from coast to coast; in eastern North America from Nova Scotia and Ontario south to Virginia and Texas; winters in South America.

Family Hirundinidae: Swallows 76

PURPLE MARTIN *Progne subis* 8 inches

Male, blue black; female, dull black and grayish.

These large, jolly swallows are commonly seen about cities and towns. Originally they dwelt in hollow trees, as some still do, but the majority now live in houses built especially for them or in cornices of dwellings or barns. Martin "houses" often consist of cunningly fashioned gabled structures atop a twelve-foot pole on lawns, but the birds are as well satisfied with soapboxes or dried gourds with holes in the side. They are most useful in keeping down the insect population.

Note: A varied, grating warble or twitter, more forcible than melodious. **Nest:** Of straw, paper, rags, et cetera, in birdhouses, gables, or hollow trees; four dull white eggs, .98 x .72. **Range:** North America, breeding from the Gulf to New Brunswick and Saskatchewan; winters in Brazil.

GRAY JAY *Perisoreus canadensis* 11½ inches

Adults suggest chickadees of abnormal size. Young are dark slate gray, nearly black on the head. These jays are well known in the northern woods, where their mischievous pranks often enliven the day for hunters, trappers, campers, and lumbermen. They show no fear of man and do not hesitate to enter camps or canoes to take what they can find—matches and trinkets as well as bacon, beans, and soap. Some of the food is cached in crevices in trees, but when necessary the birds live without the help of man, feeding on insects, buds, seeds, and fruit. The Gray Jay has many names. "Whisky Jack," "Camp Robber," and "Moosebird" are among the commonest.
  Note: A harsh *ca-ca-ca;* other typical jay sounds. **Nest:** Usually at low elevations in coniferous trees; of twigs, moss, and feathers; four grayish eggs, 1.15 x .80, specked with brown. **Range:** North America from northern United States north to the limit of trees and southward in western mountains.

Family Corvidae: Jays, Crows, et cetera 78

BLUE JAY *Cyanocitta cristata* 11¾ inches

These are among our best-known and most beautiful birds, but their reputation is not good. They rob other birds of their eggs and nestlings and they sometimes make serious inroads on fruit crops, but they are not as bad as they are painted. Most of their food consists of insects and wild berries and nuts, and their habit of burying acorns and beechnuts gives them some importance as tree planters. Even if they were worse than they are, their flashing color could not be spared from the winter landscape.

Voice: Harsh, discordant screams, melodious whistles; a musical song and a variety of other notes. Excellent mimic. Very noisy. **Nest:** Of twigs and sticks, lined with softer material; placed in a bush or tree, ten to fifteen feet aboveground; four pale greenish-blue eggs, 1.10 x .80, specked with brown. **Range:** Permanent resident of eastern North America; northernmost birds move southward in winter.

79 Family Corvidae: Jays, Crows, et cetera

SCRUB JAY *Aphelocoma coerulescens* 11½ inches

In the eastern states this species is found only in Florida and as a rule only in scrub-oak areas. It is quite readily distinguished from the Florida race of the Blue Jay, which inhabits the same territory, since it has no crest and no white marks on the wings and tail and its back is brown instead of blue. Diet is similar to that of the Blue Jay—insects and other animal food (including at times the eggs and nestlings of other birds), acorns, seeds, and berries—but much more feeding is done on the ground.

Voice: A harsh call similar to the Blue Jay's; a variety of other notes and calls. **Nest:** A flat, compact structure of sticks and twigs; lined with softer material; placed in a bush or scrub oak not far aboveground; three or four bluish- or greenish-white eggs, 1.05 x .80, with brown spots. **Range:** Mostly western North America; in eastern United States found only in Florida, where it is irregularly distributed through scrub-oak sections.

Family Corvidae: Jays, Crows, et cetera   80

GREEN JAY *Xanthoura luxuosa* 12 inches

Also known as the Rio Grande Jay. These beautiful birds, like other members of the family, sometimes feed on the eggs and nestlings of other birds, but they also take quantities of insects. In winter they turn to wild seeds, grain, berries, and nuts. Dense thickets in dry areas are the preferred habitat, but the birds also appear around farm buildings and other settlements, where their presence seldom goes unnoticed; they are very noisy and aggressive.

Voice: Similar to that of other jays; many calls, whistles, and imitations. **Nest:** Loosely made of twigs, lined with grass, rootlets, hair, et cetera; not easily found, as it is usually hidden in a dense thicket at some distance from the ground; four grayish eggs, 1.05 x .80, profusely spotted with brown and lilac, especially at the large end. **Range:** Fairly common in the Lower Rio Grande Valley in southern Texas; occurs through Mexico to northern South America.

81 Family Corvidae: Jays, Crows, et cetera

BLACK-BILLED MAGPIE *Pica pica* 20 inches

This handsome member of the crow family is sure to attract attention, not only because of its striking appearance and noisy scolding but also because of its pert ways and thieving habits. The long tail makes flight laborious in a high wind, and at such times the birds are usually very quiet. They feed chiefly on large insects but also take small animals, fruits, and grain.

Note: A loud, harsh *cack, cack* and an endless variety of whistles and imitations. **Nest:** A large, globular heap of sticks placed in bushes or trees four to fifty feet from the ground; entrance is at one side, and the interior is lined with grass and mud; four to six white eggs, 1.25 x .90, thickly specked with yellowish brown. Loose nesting colonies are formed. **Range:** Western North America, east to the plains, north to Alaska. In winter stragglers come as far east as Michigan and Illinois.

Family Corvidae: Jays, Crows, et cetera 82

COMMON RAVEN *Corvus corax* (BELOW) 25 inches

Habits of ravens and crows are nearly identical. All at times are very destructive to young birds and eggs and to cultivated crops. Common Ravens, largest of the group, are found in the mountains from Georgia and on the coast from Maine northward.

WHITE-NECKED RAVEN *Corvus cryptoleucus*
18½ inches
The white bases of the neck feathers are visible when the feathers are ruffed up. Southwestern United States.

AMERICAN CROW *Corvus brachyrhynchos* (ABOVE)
19 inches
The common crow of North America; very well known.

FISH CROW *Corvus ossifragus* 16 inches
A small species, very similar to the American Crow but with a more nasal, croaking voice; found on the Atlantic Coast north to Massachusetts.

83 Family Corvidae: Jays, Crows, et cetera

BLACK-CAPPED CHICKADEE *Parus atricapillus* (ABOVE) 5¼ inches

Because of their uniform good nature even in the coldest weather and their confiding dispositions at all times, chickadees are among our most popular birds. They are common about farms, shady suburbs, and woodland edges, and in both city and country they come to feeding stations provided with suet, sunflower seeds, or peanut butter. In the wild their food consists largely of insects, their eggs and pupae, but they also eat seeds and berries and can survive through long spells of sub-zero weather.

Note: *Chick-a-dee-dee-dee* or simply *dee-dee;* a clear, whistled *phe-be;* scolding and chuckling notes. **Nest:** In a hollow in a decaying stump or tree; six to eight white eggs, .60 x .48, sparingly dotted with reddish brown. **Range:** Eastern North America, breeding in northern United States and northward, and south in the mountains to North Carolina. The Carolina Chickadee (*carolinensis*) (ILLUSTRATED BELOW) is found in southeastern United States, breeding north to New Jersey and Ohio.

Family Paridae: Titmice 84

BROWN-CAPPED CHICKADEE *Parus hudsonicus* 5 inches

In shape, size, and habits this little northerner is very like the Black-capped Chickadee, but its cap is brown, its back brownish gray, and its whitish under parts shade into brown on the flanks and sides. The black throat and the white facial area are almost identical in the two species. The Brown-capped seldom deserts spruce or other coniferous forests, but is very tame, especially around lumbermen's camps. It is met with in the United States only on the northern border or at elevations above three thousand feet, though winter stragglers may turn up as far south as New Jersey.

Note: Very much like that of the Black-capped Chickadee, but slower and uttered more incessantly. **Nest:** In cavities in stumps, trees, posts, or poles; lined with grass, feathers, and fur; six or seven white eggs, .60 x .46, sprinkled with brown. **Range:** Northern border of United States north to the limit of trees.

85   Family Paridae: Titmice

TUFTED TITMOUSE *Parus bicolor* (ABOVE) 6 inches

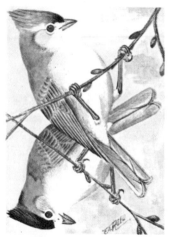

Gray back, head crested, forehead black, flanks brownish. The habits of these larger titmice are almost identical with those of chickadees. They swing from the ends of twigs in all manner of positions and creep about tree trunks, peering into the crevices of the bark for insects. They are common in the southern states, breeding from the Gulf to New York and Illinois; resident throughout their range.

Note: Loud, clear, persistent whistles. **Nest:** In hollow stumps and branches, lined with feathers and down; five or six white eggs, .73 x .65, finely spotted with brown. **Range:** From New Jersey to Illinois south to Florida and the Gulf Coast. The similar Black-crested Titmouse (*atricristatus*) (ILLUSTRATED BELOW), which has a white forehead and rusty flanks, is found in southern and western Texas. The birds are very tame, especially during the breeding season, when they allow themselves to be lifted from the nest by hand.

Family Paridae: Titmice 86

WHITE-BREASTED NUTHATCH *Sitta carolinensis* 6 inches

Male with crown bluish black; female with the crown gray; both sexes have white tail patches and chestnut under tail coverts.

These little bluish-gray birds are most commonly observed clambering down tree trunks head first. They feed chiefly on insect eggs and pupae, but they also take seeds and small fruits and are easily attracted to feeding stations if sunflower seeds, peanut hearts, and suet are provided.

Note: A nasal *yank-yank* and a repeated *ya-ya,* all in the same tone. **Nest:** In a cavity, often in decayed wood, in the trunk or branch of a tree; filled with leaves and usually lined with feathers; five or six white eggs, .75 x .55, spotted with reddish brown. **Range:** From coast to coast; in eastern North America from southern Canada to Florida, the Gulf Coast, and Mexico; resident throughout most of this area in woodlands, orchards, and shady villages.

87 Family Sittidae: Nuthatches

RED-BREASTED NUTHATCH *Sitta canadensis* 4½ inches

Smaller than the White-breasted Nuthatch and with rustier under parts; black stripe through the eye. In habits these birds are very similar to the White-breasted, but they are often found in flocks, whereas the White-breasteds are usually found in pairs, accompanied by their young in the fall. Red-breasteds prefer coniferous trees, where they feed on seeds as well as on the insects, eggs, and grubs under the bark.

Note: A nasal *yank-yank* not so loud as that of the White-breasted and usually repeated more often. **Nest:** In a cavity in a dead stump or limb, with the opening area nearly always smeared with pitch or balsam; lined with grasses and feathers; four to seven white eggs, .60 x .50, very thickly spotted with reddish brown. **Range:** North America, breeding in evergreen forests from the northern parts of the northern tier of states, northward and southward in the mountains; winters south nearly to the Gulf and southern California.

Family Sittidae: Nuthatches 88

BROWN-HEADED NUTHATCH *Sitta pusilla* 4¼ inches

Crown brownish; white patch on the nape.

These diminutive nuthatches are found in the southern states, where their favored habitat·is open pinewoods. They nest very early, commencing the excavation of their holes in January and having complete sets of eggs by the middle of February. They are usually found in small flocks and in the late evening can often be observed flying to the top of a pine, where they sleep all huddled together. They feed on insects and eggs along the bark of a tree and they also eat pine mast.

Note: A continued twittering *nya-nya*. **Nest:** In cavities in dead limbs or stumps, sometimes only a few inches from the ground or again as high up as fifty feet; five or six white eggs, .62 x .49, with numerous spots of reddish brown. **Range:** South Atlantic and Gulf states, breeding north to southern Delaware; appears irregularly somewhat farther north.

89 Family Sittidae: Nuthatches

BROWN CREEPER *Certhia familiaris* 5½ inches

Tail feathers stiffened and pointed; rump rusty; bill curved.

This odd and inconspicuous little bird is most often observed creeping up the trunk of a tree in a spiral, methodically investigating bark crevices for larvae or grubs. When it has finished one tree it drops to the foot of the next and continues as before. The birds are fairly common in most wooded areas, including suburban streets with mature trees. They are quite tame and allow close approach before flying away.

Voice: A very faint trill; a weak *tseep*, hardly audible except at close range. **Nest:** Of twigs, moss, and bark; placed behind loose bark on trees or stumps, usually not far aboveground; six white eggs, .58 x .48, specked with reddish brown. **Range:** Breeds from coast to coast; in eastern North America from northern New England (farther south in mountains) and Minnesota northward; winters in southern United States.

Family Certhiidae: Creepers 90

HOUSE WREN *Troglodytes aëdon* 4¾ inches

Brownish above with tail and wings barred; dull grayish below with brown-barred flanks; tail often cocked. These bold, sociable, confiding birds seem to prefer the vicinity of man, for though they build nests in woodland trees, they more often take orchard or shade trees or bird boxes or niches in buildings. Their food consists wholly of small insects, and they should be welcomed in every yard and garden.

Song: Loud, clear, and bubbling over with enthusiasm; an emphatic, scolding chatter, amusing in a bird of its size. **Nest:** Of grass or weeds, stuffed into any crevice that takes the birds' fancy, often in bird boxes or in holes in orchard trees; six white eggs, .64 x .52, so minutely and thickly dotted with pinkish brown that the ground color is almost obscured. **Range:** Breeds from coast to coast; in the East from southeastern Canada south to Kentucky, South Carolina, and Texas; winters in South Atlantic states and along the Gulf Coast.

91 Family Troglodytidae: Wrens

WINTER WREN   *Troglodytes troglodytes*   4 inches

Bright cinnamon above, paler below; heavily barred wings, tail, and belly; stubby tail often cocked.

In most of the United States these short, stoutly built little wrens are seen only in winter. They are quite secretive and very difficult to drive out of the brush heaps and tangles which they inhabit. Even in a small brush pile the birds, at the approach of man, will run from side to side in the interior instead of flying out.

Song: A rippling flow of melody, more musical than that of the House Wren but not so loud. **Nest:** In brush heaps, tin cans, hollow stumps, or in crevices in unoccupied buildings; made of piles of grass, weeds, et cetera, and lined with feathers; five white eggs, .65 x .50, sparingly specked with reddish brown. **Range:** Breeds in boreal region of the Northern Hemisphere; in North America from the northern edge of the United States northward; winters in the southern part of the breeding range and southward to the Gulf.

Family Troglodytidae: Wrens   92

BEWICK'S WREN   *Thryomanes bewickii*   5 inches

Dark brown above, whitish below; whitish line over the eye; tail relatively long, with white tips on the outer feathers.

Like all wrens, these seem to be very nervous as they move restlessly about brush heaps, along stone walls, and over fallen trees and stumps. They feed on insects, nearly always close to the ground. They are abundant in parts of the Midwest, in some sections replacing the House Wren. Like the House Wren, they often build their nests in the vicinity of man.

Voice: A sweet chant of liquid, melodious notes; low, buzzy alarm calls. **Nest:** In holes in trees, in bird boxes, in crevices in barns and sheds—almost anywhere; made of straw, grass, and trash; five to seven white eggs, .66 x .50, profusely specked with brown. **Range:** From coast to coast; east of the plains breeds from central Alabama and Louisiana north to South Dakota and Michigan; moves southward in winter.

93   Family Troglodytidae: Wrens

CAROLINA WREN *Thryothorus ludovicianus* 5½ inches

Largest of eastern wrens; rusty brownish red above, whitish, washed with rusty, below; rusty bars on wings and tail; sharply defined white stripe over eye. Brush heaps and woodland thickets and tangles are the preferred habitats, the species appearing less often around human dwellings than the House Wren and Bewick's. The tail, which is commonly held erect as the bird sits or flits about in the brush, is held downward when it sings. The flight, usually for short distances only, is accomplished with rapid wingbeats and a jerking motion of the tail.

Song: Loud and tinkling, often in units of three syllables. **Nest:** In brush heaps, washbasins, in holes in trees, in bushes or bird boxes; of weeds, grass, and trash; five to seven white eggs, .74 x .60, spotted with brown. **Range:** Eastern United States, breeding from Florida and the Gulf north to New York and Illinois and west to central Texas.

Family Troglodytidae: Wrens 94

CACTUS WREN *Campylorhynchus brunneicapillus* 8½ inches

Much larger than eastern wrens; white throat and breast marked with black; white line over the eye; outer tail feathers barred with black and white. Has the wrenlike habit of cocking its tail but, like the Carolina Wren, hangs the tail and raises the head when singing. Cactus groves are the special haunts of these birds. They are quite social, and several pairs may nest in the same small thicket; but since each pair is likely to have two or three dummy nests, they are not always so abundant as they seem.

Song: "Unwren-like" (Finley); scolding notes. **Nest:** In cactus or other thorny shrub; very large, purse-shaped, with the entrance at the side; made of thorny twigs and grasses woven together and lined with feathers; four or five creamy white eggs, .95 x .65, finely sprinkled with reddish brown. **Range:** Southwestern border of the United States southward into Mexico, ranging from southern Texas to California.

95 Family Troglodytidae: Wrens

SEDGE WREN *Cistothorus platensis* (ABOVE)   4 inches

This species can be distinguished from the next by its streaked crown. These shy creatures inhabit wet, grassy meadows. They attach their small globular nests to the living stalks of grass or sedge, and the nests rise higher and higher as the season advances. Usually they are well concealed. Many dummy nests are constructed. The eggs are pure white.

MARSH WREN *Telmatodytes palustris* (BELOW) 5 inches

Note the long, curved bill and the white stripe over the eye. The "Cattail Wren" is a bird of the coastal marshes and the reedy banks of sluggish streams. The woven nests are attached to the stems of tall marsh plants. Dummy nests are built. The eggs are profusely dotted with brown. Breeds from coast to coast; in eastern North America from the Gulf to Massachusetts and Manitoba.

Family Troglodytidae: Wrens   96

ROCK WREN *Salpinctes obsoletus* 5¾ inches

Upper parts stone color, specked with black; rump brownish; under parts whitish with indistinct dark streaks on the throat and breast.

These birds are common in the dry foothills of the Rockies and westward. They are well named, for they live among the rocks, continuously hunting in the crevices for insects and spiders. Their color blends with the background, and since they have a habit of slipping into holes and crevices they are quite difficult to see.

Song: Varied, at times canarylike; harsh, grating call note. **Nest:** Of pebbles, rock flakes, sticks, weeds, and grass; concealed in crevices or burrows and lined with soft material; five or six white eggs, .72 x .54, sparingly specked with reddish brown. **Range:** Western United States from central Texas and the western border of the plains to the Pacific, north to Dakota and British Columbia; winters from southwestern United States southward.

97 Family Troglodytidae: Wrens

MOCKINGBIRD *Mimus polyglottos* 10½ inches

General colors, pale gray above, white below; the white patches on the wings and tail are very conspicuous in flight.

This is the most celebrated vocalist of the South and is considered by many the most versatile singer in North America. Others believe that the song of the Brown Thrasher is more musical, but there is no doubt that the "Mocker" excels in mimicking the other sounds of its environment, not necessarily those made by birds. It frequents gardens, fields, and open woods; lives on fruits and berries and insects.

Song: An indescribable medley, usually of brilliant virtuosity, sometimes harsh and unpleasant. **Nest:** Generally in impenetrable thickets, though often in more open places; of twigs and trash lined with rootlets; four or five blue-green eggs, .95 x .70, blotched with reddish brown. **Range:** Southern United States, breeding north to New Jersey and Ohio.

Family Mimidae: Mimic Thrushes 98

CATBIRD *Dumetella carolinensis* 9 inches

A slender dark gray bird with a black cap and chestnut under tail coverts.

Catbirds are abundant in gardens, swamps, and scrubby pastures. They are persistent singers, with a large repertoire of their own, and are quite skillful at imitating the notes of other birds. Their song, which they delight in rendering for an hour or more at a time from a perch in a tree or bush, is an extraordinary medley, interspersed with mews and catcalls. Feeding and other habits are similar to the Mockingbird's.

Voice: Song, a medley like the Mockingbird's; individual phrases are seldom repeated; mews and catcalls. **Nest:** In dense hedges and thickets; of twigs, rootlets, and grass, lined with finer material; four plain greenish-blue eggs, .95 x .70. **Range:** Eastern North America, breeding from the Gulf to Nova Scotia and southern Manitoba; rare west of the Rockies; winters in the southern states.

99 Family Mimidae: Mimic Thrushes

BROWN THRASHER *Toxostoma rufum* 11½ inches

Bright reddish brown above, with white wing bars; white below, heavily streaked with brown; long, curved bill; long tail.

Taken as a whole, the song of this thrasher is one of the most musical and pleasing—perhaps the most so—in the bird world. It is similar to those of the Mockingbird and the Catbird but is without the harsh notes that mar their performances. It is usually delivered from a high perch in a tree, and each phrase is repeated. The birds live on insects and grain and generally feed on or near the ground.

Song: A clear, sweet carol, often long continued; a prolonged whistle. **Nest:** Of twigs and rootlets, in hedges, thickets, and thornbushes; four or five bluish-white eggs, 1.08 x .80, finely dotted with reddish brown. **Range:** Eastern North America, breeding from the Gulf to southern Canada; winters in the southern half of the United States.

Family Mimidae: Mimic Thrushes 100

SAGE THRASHER *Oreoscoptes montanus* 8¾ inches

Much smaller than the Brown Thrasher; short, slender bill; white tips on outer tail feathers; streaked throat, breast, and sides.

This species is often known as the "Mountain Mockingbird" because of the brilliance of its song, which includes the notes of many other birds. It inhabits sagebrush regions and is partial to the plains, though not infrequently met with in open mountains. It feeds on insects and small fruits.

Song: A varied performance, long continued. **Nest:** In bushes, especially sage and cactus; a loose structure of bark strips, small twigs, and coarse grasses, lined with fine rootlets; three or four eggs, .95 x .70, with bright reddish-brown spots over a rich greenish-blue ground. **Range:** Sagebrush regions of western United States from the plains to the Pacific and east to Texas; winters in Mexico and Lower California.

101 Family Mimidae: Mimic Thrushes

AMERICAN ROBIN *Turdus migratorius* 10 inches

Probably the best-known and best-loved bird in eastern North America, its joyous song is accepted as the official opening of spring. It lives on intimate terms with man, nesting near homes, patrolling lawns for worms, and watching trees and fields for ripening fruits and berries. The American Robin is really a thrush; it was miscalled after the Robin Redbreast of the Old World, which is more like our bluebirds. Females are duller than males, the young intermediate between the two and with spotted breasts. The spots disappear in the first molt.

Song: A loud, cheery carol, often long continued. **Nest:** A coarse, substantial structure of mud and grass; placed on horizontal boughs or forks in bushes and trees and in all sorts of odd places about dwellings; four or five blue-green eggs, 1.15 x .80. **Range:** Breeds over the greater part of North America, wintering farther south, though some birds remain as far north as southern New England.

Family Turdidae: Thrushes 102

WOOD THRUSH *Hylocichla mustelina*   8 inches

Reddish brown above, brightest on the head; white under parts heavily marked with round spots.

These thrushes are locally abundant in swamps and moist woodlands and in shady residential areas. They are among our best songsters, their tones being very rich and flutelike. Like most thrushes, they are most often heard along toward night. Much of their food is obtained by scratching in dry leaves on the ground.

Song: Very clear and flutelike, containing many notes of the scale; often two or more birds answer back and forth from different parts of an area; calls, a sharp *quit, quit* and a liquid *quirt*. **Nest:** In bushes or trees, usually not more than ten feet from the ground; of grass, weeds, leaves, and some mud; three or four blue-green eggs, 1.02 x .75. **Range:** Eastern United States, breeding from central New Hampshire and southeastern Ontario south to northern Florida and Louisiana; winters south of United States.

103 Family Turdidae: Thrushes

HERMIT THRUSH *Hylocichla guttata* 7 inches

The reddish-brown tail, much deeper in color than the back and head, is the field mark of the Hermit Thrush. The Fox Sparrow has a reddish tail, but its shape, its typical sparrow bill, and its more heavily marked under parts distinguish it from any thrush. The Hermit's practice of slowly raising and lowering its tail helps to separate it from other thrushes. Feeding habits are similar to the Wood Thrush's, but the Hermit is less apt to make its home near human dwellings.

Voice: A clear, flutelike song with the sweetness and purity of tone of the Wood Thrush's, but more varied and less powerful; often with a ventriloquial effect; cluck calls and scolding notes. **Nest:** Of fibers, leaves, and rootlets, lined with softer material; usually on the ground under a hummock or the spreading branch of an evergreen; four greenish-blue eggs, .85 x .65. **Range:** Breeds from northern United States northward and southward in the mountains; winters in southern states.

Family Turdidae: Thrushes 104

GRAY-CHEEKED THRUSH *Hylocichla minima* (ABOVE) 7½ inches

Similar to the following, but with the indistinct eye ring white and the cheeks and breast pale gray instead of buffy. Breeds in northern Canada and Alaska and south through the mountains of New York and New England; migrates through the eastern states to Central and South America. The subspecies Bicknell's Gray-cheeked Thrush (*bicknelli*) is the form which breeds in Nova Scotia and the higher mountains of the northeastern states.

OLIVE-BACKED THRUSH *Hylocichla ustulata* (BELOW) 7¼ inches

Upper parts olive gray with brownish tinge; breast, eye ring and sides of head buff; only by close observation can it be distinguished in the field from the Gray-cheeked Thrush. The song is similar to the Veery's. Breeds from northern United States to New Brunswick and southward in the mountains; winters south of United States.

105 Family Turdidae: Thrushes

VEERY *Hylocichla fuscescens* 7½ inches

Entire upper parts a uniform tawny or reddish brown, soiled white below, with a few faint marks on the breast; least spotted of all thrushes.

This species is abundant in swamp and bottom lands and in open woods, especially in places where ferns grow luxuriantly, but it is also found in dry upland pastures. It feeds on the forest floor on insects, seeds, and wild fruit.

Song: Very peculiar, not nearly so melodious as that of the Wood Thrush, but still attractive; a slightly descending *too-whe-u-whe-u-whe-u* not unlike a long unwinding of its own name; a clear *whee-you* call. **Nest:** On the ground among leaves, in mossy hummocks, or under small bushes or in tangled masses of briers; made of strips of bark, leaves, fibers, and moss; four greenish-blue eggs, .88 x .65. **Range:** Eastern North America, breeding in the northern half of the United States and southern Canada; winters in Central and South America.

Family Turdidae: Thrushes 106

EASTERN BLUEBIRD *Sialia sialis* 7 inches

Male, bright blue above, with chestnut throat and breast; female, rather gray above, with most of the blue in the wings and tail; young, spotted with white above, with brown on the breast.

Eastern Bluebirds have always been associated with farmyards and orchards and open woodlands, but since the advent of the House Sparrow and the Common Starling they have had to meet stiff competition for nesting sites. Conservationists suggest erecting bird boxes with an opening no wider than one and one quarter inches. These should be placed on poles less than eight feet aboveground, near cover and open lawn or field.

Song: A short, sweet warble, faintly querulous. **Nest:** In holes in trees, in bird boxes, and in crannies about buildings; lined with grasses; four or five pale bluish eggs, .84 x 62. **Range:** Eastern North America, breeding from the Gulf to New Brunswick and Manitoba; winters in southern United States.

107 Family Turdidae: Thrushes

WHEATEAR *Oenanthe oenanthe* 6 inches

This is a bird of the Arctic, accidental in northeastern North America and, occasionally, much farther south along the coast. The birds are brown above, lighter brown below. The white rump and the black-and-white tail are the best field marks. Wheatears spend most of their time on the ground and are usually found in barren, open country, where they hop about restlessly as they feed on insects and their larvae and on berries, fruits, and seeds.

Voice: Harsh call note; short warble. **Nest:** Of grasses, hair, and rubbish; hidden in the innermost crevices among rocks, in deserted Bank Swallow nests, rabbit burrows, et cetera; four to six unmarked pale greenish-blue eggs, .94 x .60. **Range:** Breeds in Greenland and in the eastern sections of the North American Arctic; winters in southern Europe; accidental in southern Canada and United States.

BLUE-GRAY GNATCATCHER *Polioptila caerulea* 5 inches

This tiny inhabitant of birdland has been compared with the Mockingbird and the Catbird for shape; with kinglets and chickadees for size; with the Cerulean Warbler for color; with the American Redstart for nervousness; with wrens for tail cocking; and with hummingbirds for daintiness in nest building. Yet there is little danger of mistaking a Blue-gray Gnatcatcher for anything else. It feeds on insects, usually in the tops of tall trees.

Song: A thin, sweet warble. **Nest:** One of the most beautiful examples of bird architecture; placed on horizontal limbs of trees at medium heights; made of plant fibers, woolly substances, and cobwebs, adorned with lichens; the walls are high, and when the bird sits, only the tail is visible; four or five bluish-white eggs, .56 x .44, specked with reddish brown. **Range:** From coast to coast; in eastern United States breeds north to New Jersey and Illinois; winters from South Carolina and the Gulf Coast southward.

109 Family Sylviidae: Gnatcatchers and Kinglets

GOLDEN-CROWNED KINGLET   *Regulus satrapa*   4 inches

Male with orange crown bordered with black; female with similar yellow crown; white stripe over the eye. Although very small, these birds are quite rugged, able to endure the severe storms and low temperatures of our northern states apparently with little concern, for they always seem happy as they flit about evergreens and underbrush for insects, eggs, and larvae. In winter they are apt to appear in small flocks, often with chickadees and nuthatches.

Song: A few weak chips, chirps, and trills. **Nest:** A large ball of soft green mosses and feathers, suspended from small twigs in the tops of coniferous trees; neatly hollowed out for the reception of six to nine creamy white eggs, .56 x .44, minutely but profusely specked with brown. **Range:** North America, breeding from northern United States northward and farther south in mountain ranges; winters throughout the United States.

Family Sylviidae: Gnatcatchers and Kinglets   110

RUBY-CROWNED KINGLET *Regulus calendula* 4¼ inches

The male's scarlet crown patch (lacking in the female) is seldom visible in the field unless the bird is angry or disturbed. Both sexes have the white eye ring. Like the Golden-crowned, these kinglets appear in the United States chiefly in winter, except along the northern border, where some of them nest. They do not remain in the North during really severe weather, but pass on to the southern half of our country.

Song: A clear, musical warble, surprisingly loud for so small a bird; call, a grating chatter. **Nest:** A ball of moss, grass, and feathers, deeply cupped; partially suspended among the small twigs at the top of a conifer, usually a spruce; very similar to the nest of the Golden-crowned; the eight white eggs, .55 x .43, are also similar but not so profusely specked. **Range:** North America, breeding northward from the northern boundary of the United States and farther south in the mountains; winters in southern half of United States.

111 Family Sylviidae: Gnatcatchers and Kinglets

WATER PIPIT *Anthus spinoletta* (ABOVE) 6½ inches

These are Arctic birds that spend the winter months in the United States southward from New Jersey and Ohio. We find them in flocks along roadsides, in fields, and along the seacoast, feeding upon weed seeds. They walk instead of hopping and constantly wag their tails. They are shy and take wing readily, uttering sharp whistles as they wheel about in the air.

SPRAGUE'S PIPIT *Anthus spragueii* (BELOW)
6¼ inches

These birds are paler than the Water Pipit. Both species have white outer tail feathers, but their walking and tail wagging and their thin bills distinguish them from the similarly marked Vesper Sparrow. Sprague's Pipit resembles the European Skylark in its way of soaring to a great height while singing. The song is very melodious, somewhat like a Bobolink's.

Family Motacillidae: Pipits 112

GREATER WAXWING *Bombycilla garrulus* 8 inches

Larger and grayer than our common Cedar Waxwing;
has yellow and white on the wing; under tail coverts
rusty. These are birds of the North, nesting to within the
Arctic Circle and appearing casually in winter in the
United States. They are found in flocks, roving restlessly
about the country, often turning up where least expected
and utterly deserting their previous haunts. They feed
chiefly on wild fruits and berries.

Voice: A lisping note similar to the Cedar Waxwing's
but rougher. **Nest:** Of small twigs and moss, lined with
feathers; usually placed at low elevations in spruce or
other conifers; eggs, 1.00 x .70, dull bluish white, sparingly specked with black, similar to those of the Cedar
Waxwing but larger. Comparatively few of their nests
have been found. **Range:** Northern parts of the Northern
Hemisphere, breeding to within the Arctic Circle and
wintering casually south to Massachusetts, Pennsylvania,
Kansas, and California.

113 Family Bombycillidae: Waxwings

CEDAR WAXWING   *Bombycilla cedrorum*   7 inches

Plumage satiny with a general brownish tone, shading to gray on the rump; crested. Waxwings are named from the curious waxlike appendages attached to the tips of the secondaries and rarely to the tail feathers. They are very sociable and usually feed in flocks, which, after the nesting season, may consist of a hundred or more birds. They are great gluttons and often eat until they can literally eat no more. Because of their fondness for cherries and cedar berries, they are known as "Cherry Birds" or "Cedar Birds."

Voice: An insignificant lisping hiss. **Nest:** A substantial structure of twigs, mosses, twine, et cetera, lined with fine grasses; usually at low elevations in orchard trees or in trees at the edge of the forest; four or five dull bluish-white eggs, .85 x .60, specked with black. **Range:** North America, breeding from Georgia, Kansas, and northern California to the Gulf of St. Lawrence and Manitoba; winters throughout eastern United States.

Family Bombycillidae: Waxwings   114

GRAY SHRIKE *Lanius excubitor* 10 inches

This shrike is larger than any other of the species found in the United States, and the breast is faintly barred. Shrikes are rapacious birds, feeding upon insects, mice, lizards, and small birds. Since their feet are made for perching, they are unable to hold their prey while tearing it apart. They impale it on barbs on a wire fence or on thorns and pull it to pieces with their hooked bills, hence the common name of "Butcher Bird." They are often observed watching from treetop perches or posts.

Song: Loud snatches consisting of various whistles and imitations suggesting the notes of a Catbird. **Nest:** Rude, bulky structures of twigs and weeds; placed in thorny trees or hedges; four to six grayish-white eggs, 1.08 x .80, with spots of light brown and darker gray. **Range:** North America, breeding chiefly in the northern parts of Canada; winters south to Virginia, Kentucky, New Mexico, and northern California.

LOGGERHEAD SHRIKE *Lanius ludovicianus* 9 inches

Similar to the Gray Shrike but pure white below, and the black mask meets over the base of the bill. The general coloration is somewhat like the mockingbird's, but this species is much more heavily built and has a strong hooked bill.

These shrikes have the same destructive habits as the northern species, yet all shrikes are of considerable benefit to mankind because of the insects and mice they kill. Loggerheads like open country with poles, trees, and wires for lookout perches.

Note: Harsh, discordant whistles. **Nest:** Of twigs, weeds, leaves, et cetera, lined with soft material; placed in scrubby hedges and thickets; four to seven grayish-white eggs, .96 x .72, spotted with brown and gray. **Range:** Breeds from coast to coast and from southern New England and Manitoba south to Florida and the Gulf Coast; winters from Virginia and southern Missouri southward.

Family Laniidae: Shrikes 116

COMMON STARLING *Sturnus vulgaris* 8½ inches

Plumage metallic green and purple, heavily spotted above and below with buffy or white; spots more noticeable in fall and early winter; bill yellow in spring, dark in winter.

Spreading out from an introduction into Central Park in New York City in 1890, these European birds are now found over most of the United States, flourishing in cities (where they sometimes prove a nuisance) and in pastures, fields, and wastelands. Their chunky bodies and short legs make them seem very awkward as they walk along the ground picking up insects and grain. Except during the nesting season, they move in flocks, the operations of which in the air are remarkably beautiful.

Voice: A long whistle; many other notes and many imitations of other birds. **Nest:** In a hole in a tree or a crevice in a building; four or five pale blue eggs, 1.15 x .85. **Range:** United States, mainly east of the Rocky Mountains, and southern Canada; still spreading.

117 Family Sturnidae: Starlings

BLACK-CAPPED VIREO *Vireo atricapillus* 4½ inches

Male with crown and sides of head glossy black, lores and eye ring white; two wing bars. Female is gray where the male is black.

This comparatively rare vireo frequents brushwood and scrub in semi-arid country. Like most vireos, it is difficult to see and is usually located by its voice. It is more active than other members of its family, but not so much so as a warbler. Its food consists largely of insects.

Song: Varied and harsh; harsh alarm note. **Nest:** Suspended from forked branches at a low elevation in a bush or small tree; made of fibers and bark strips closely woven together with spider webs and sometimes decorated on the outside with lichens, bits of wood and paper; four white eggs, .70 x .52, unmarked. **Range:** Breeds from central and western Texas north to southern Kansas; winters in Mexico.

Family Vireonidae: Vireos 118

WHITE-EYED VIREO *Vireo griseus* 5 inches

Olive green above, with two yellowish wing bars; white below, with a yellowish wash at the sides; yellow spectacles around a white eye. Bell's Vireo (*bellii*) is quite similar but has narrow white spectacles and a dark eye. White-eyed Vireos show partiality for low, swampy thickets and tangled masses of vines or blackberry bushes. In addition to insects, they feed on wild fruits and berries, especially in winter.

Note: A great variety of clear whistles and squeaky notes; harsh mews; loud, emphatic song. **Nest:** A bulky structure of strips of bark, leaves, paper, et cetera; either placed in crotched branches or partially suspended in a fork in a low bush or tree; four white eggs, .75 x .55, scattered with minute brown specks. **Range:** Breeds from Massachusetts and Manitoba to the Gulf; winters in South Carolina and along the Gulf Coast and southward.

YELLOW-THROATED VIREO *Vireo flavifrons* 5¾ inches

Upper parts greenish; throat, breast, and spectacles yellow; two prominent white wing bars.

This is a handsome bird of the leafy tops of tall trees in open deciduous woodlands, orchards, and shady residential areas. In habits and song it is very similar to the Red-eyed Vireo but seems not to be so abundant. It is, however, probably much more abundant than many suppose. The difficulty of getting a clear look at the yellow breast when the bird is high in the trees and the similarity of the song in the two species cause much confusion.

Song: Similar to that of the Red-eyed Vireo, but louder and more nasal, less varied, uttered less often. **Nest:** A pensile structure of bark strips, grasses, et cetera, often ornamented with lichens; four creamy or rosy white eggs, .82 x .60, specked with reddish brown. **Range:** Eastern North America, breeding from the Gulf to southern Canada; winters from Mexico to northern South America.

Family Vireonidae: Vireos 120

SOLITARY VIREO *Vireo solitarius* 5¾ inches

Crown and sides of head bluish slate; spectacles and throat white; back and flanks greenish yellow, darker above; two white wing bars.

One of the prettiest of the vireos, the colors being in just the right proportion and blending into perfect harmony. The birds arrive early in the spring and make their homes in woodlands, either among evergreens or deciduous trees or in mixed stands of both. They feed high and low in trees and undergrowth, their diet consisting almost wholly of insects.

Song: Similar to those of the Yellow-throated and Redeyed Vireos, but longer and more varied. Slurred notes are characteristic. **Nest:** A handsome, finely woven basket with the outside often decorated with lichens and spider webs; four white eggs, .77 x .57, with chestnut specks. **Range:** Breeds from the Canadian coast to New England, and farther south in the mountains; winters from South Carolina and the Gulf Coast southward.

121 Family Vireonidae: Vireos

RED-EYED VIREO *Vireo olivaceus* 6 inches

Olive green above, white below; crown slaty gray with a black border; white stripe above eye; eye reddish; no wing bars. The Black-whiskered Vireo (*altiloquus*) of tropical Florida and the West Indies is almost identical except for the black whisker mark. Red-eyed Vireos are more abundant than any other members of the family and are also one of the most abundant birds of the United States. All through spring and summer their monotonous warble is heard from woodland and roadside. Often during the spring migrations of warblers, Red-eyed Vireos drown out the songs of other birds.

Song: Delivered in parts, with a few seconds' intermission between; continues from morning till night, sometimes mistaken for robin; a short varied warble; a petulant mew. **Nest:** A typical vireo woven basket; four white eggs, .85 x .55, with a few blackish-brown specks. **Range:** Breeds from the Gulf to Labrador and Manitoba; winters in South America.

Family Vireonidae: Vireos 122

PHILADELPHIA VIREO *Vireo philadelphicus* (ABOVE) 5 inches

This vireo, which nests in the Far North, is more common in migration than most people realize. It is not distinctively marked (but note the yellowish breast and the lack of wing bars), it stays high in the trees, and its song is similar to that of the Red-eyed. Its nests are swung from branches at high altitudes and are not easy to find.

WARBLING VIREO *Vireo gilvus* (BELOW) 5 inches

Similar in appearance to the Philadelphia Vireo, but paler olive green above and white (occasionally with a yellowish wash) below. These are among the more common vireos. They are found in open woodlands, but in the eastern states most frequently in shade trees about farmhouses and in cities. Their song is a long-drawn-out warble after the style of the Purple Finch, very different from that of other vireos.

123 Family Vireonidae: Vireos

BLACK AND WHITE WARBLER *Mniotilta varia* 5¼ inches

Black and white striped above; male more heavily streaked with black below than the female.

These warblers are often known as "Black and White Creepers" because of their habit of creeping along the limbs and branches of trees. They are not so plodding and systematic as the Brown Creeper, which belongs to another family. They are abundant in northern United States in open woods, swamps, and even in parks, gleaning insects and grubs from the crevices in the bark of trees.

Song: A weak, thin, wiry *tsee, tsee, tsee*. **Nest:** Of grasses and strips of bark on the ground at the foot of a stump or tree trunk or beside a rock; four or five white eggs, .65 x .55, profusely spotted with reddish brown and lavender. **Range:** Breeds from Newfoundland and Manitoba south to Georgia and west to Texas and Kansas; winters from Florida southward.

Family Parulidae: Wood Warblers 124

PROTHONOTARY WARBLER *Protonotaria citrea* 5¼ inches

Head and breast intense yellow, almost orange on the head of the male; wings bluish gray; inner webs of tail feathers (except middle pair) white. Female similar but duller.

This species is found in bushy swamps and in willows on the borders of pools, lakes, and streams. They often occur where chickadees and Tree Swallows are found, all three nesting in holes in dead stubs near water. Prothonotaries are the only eastern warblers that habitually nest in tree cavities.

Song: A loud, ringing *tweet, tweet, tweet*. **Nest:** In holes in dead stubs or in deserted woodpecker holes; the hole is filled with moss, leaves, and grasses and is hollowed out at the top to receive the four to six creamy white eggs, .72 x .55, which are heavily spotted with reddish brown. **Range:** Breeds from the Gulf north to Delaware, Illinois, and Minnesota; winters in Central America.

125 Family Parulidae: Wood Warblers

SWAINSON'S WARBLER *Limnothlypis swainsonii* 5 inches

Upper parts brownish; under parts whitish; a white stripe above the eye, a brown stripe through it.

This species favors canebrakes, swamps, stagnant pools thickly overgrown with rushes and tangled vines, and bushes—places frequented by Least Bitterns and Marsh Wrens; it is also found on higher land in rhododendron thickets. It is difficult to see and for many years was believed, wrongly, to be very rare.

Song: A series of descending loud, clear whistles with a ventriloquial effect. **Nest:** Quite a large structure consisting mostly of leaves, bark, roots, and pine needles; hidden, usually at low elevations, in canebrakes, vine tangles, or bushes; four or five unmarked white or bluish-white eggs, .77 x .59. **Range:** Southeastern United States, breeding from Maryland and Indiana south to Florida and Louisiana; winters in the tropics.

Family Parulidae: Wood Warblers 126

WORM-EATING WARBLER *Helmitheros vermivorus* 5½ inches

Black stripes on a buffy head; back, wings, and tail dull olive green; buffy white below.

These birds, unlike most warblers, spend the greater part of their time on the ground. They feed on small caterpillars and are very fond of spiders, quantities of which they find by overturning bits of bark and leaves. They also glean part of their living vireo-fashion from the underside of leaves. They are met with in open, shrubby woodlands, on hillsides, and in brushy pastures.

Song: A weak, rapid chipping; a rare sunset flight song similar to the Ovenbird's. **Nest:** On the ground in a depression under a log, stone, or bush; of dead leaves and grass, lined with fine grass and hair; four or five white eggs, .70 x .55, spotted with brownish. **Range:** Eastern United States, breeding from north Georgia and southern Missouri to Connecticut and Iowa; winters in the West Indies and Central America.

127 Family Parulidae: Wood Warblers

GOLDEN-WINGED WARBLER   *Vermivora chrysoptera* (BELOW)   5 inches

Gray above, white below; yellow fore crown and wing patch; black throat; black patch on side of head. In the female the black is replaced by dark gray.

Occasionally these interesting warblers cross with the Blue-winged, producing two distinct hybrid types which have been named Brewster's and Lawrence's Warblers. Brewster's (ILLUSTRATED ABOVE), the commoner of the two, has a black line through the eye, a yellow forehead and wing bars, and a yellow breast patch, except for which the under parts are white. Its voice may be like that of either parent or a mixture of the two. The birds frequent woodland openings and brushy areas.

Song: A buzzy *zwee-ze-ze-ze.* **Nest:** Of rootlets, bark strips, and grass; on or near the ground in dense weed clumps; five white eggs, .66 x .51, speckled with brown and purple. **Range:** Breeds from Massachusetts, Illinois, and Minnesota to New Jersey, Georgia (mountains), and Iowa; winters in Central and South America.

Family Parulidae: Wood Warblers   128

BLUE-WINGED WARBLER *Vermivora pinus* (BELOW) 4¾ inches

Yellow fore crown and under parts; black line through the eye; two white wing bars.

The Lawrence-type hybrid (ILLUSTRATED ABOVE) is less common than the Brewster type (see under Golden-winged Warbler, p. 128). The Lawrence type has the white wing bars of the Blue-winged, the black throat and black face patch of the Golden-winged; fore crown and under parts are yellow. Both types of hybrids show considerable individual variation, but they nearly always conform sufficiently to be readily identifiable.

Song: A buzz in two notes, the first usually higher than the second. **Nest:** On or near the ground in dense weed clumps or blackberry vines; of leaves, grass, and plant fibers; five white eggs, .65 x .50, sparingly specked with brown. **Range:** Breeds from Massachusetts, Michigan, and Minnesota south to Maryland, Georgia (in the mountains), Kentucky, and Missouri; winters in Mexico and Central America.

129 Family Parulidae: Wood Warblers

BACHMAN'S WARBLER *Vermivora bachmanii* 4¼ inches

Olive green above; male with yellow forehead, cheeks, and under parts, black cap and black breast patch; female has gray instead of black, is less definitely marked, and duller.

This very rare species (possibly the rarest warbler in eastern United States) was first discovered near Charleston, South Carolina, by Audubon's friend, the naturalist-clergyman, Dr. John Bachman. It seeks out thickly grown swamps and bottom lands for feeding and nesting. Intensive drainage of its favored haunts may account for its scarcity.

Song: An insignificant warble or twitter, somewhat like the song of the Parula Warbler. **Nest:** In low bushes or briers, usually in dense swampland; made of grasses, stems, and leaf skeletons and lined with fibers; four pure white eggs, .63 x .48. **Range:** Has bred in Missouri, Arkansas, Kentucky, Indiana, Alabama, and South Carolina; winters in Cuba.

Family Parulidae: Wood Warblers 130

TENNESSEE WARBLER *Vermivora peregrina* 5 inches

Note the white stripe over the eye. Male has gray head, olive-green back, white under parts; female's head and back are nearly the same color and the under parts are yellowish. Fall birds are duller above, yellowish below, and the stripe above the eye is yellowish.

Its smaller size, fine, pointed bill, and nervous activity distinguish this warbler from any of the vireos. Like many of our birds, it was inappropriately named. The first specimen was taken in Tennessee, but it does not nest in that state and during migration is no more common there than elsewhere.

Song: A simple ditty somewhat like that of the Chipping Sparrow. **Nest:** Well concealed on the ground in moss or grass or under a bush or small tree; of grasses, lined with finer grasses or hair; five or six white eggs, .62 x .45, speckled with reddish brown and lilac. **Range:** Breeds from the northern parts of the northern tier of states northward; winters in Central and South America.

131 Family Parulidae: Wood Warblers

Books in the DOUBLEDAY NATURE GUIDES series you will want to add to your nature library

NORTH AMERICAN GAME FISHES—FRANCESCA LA MONTE. ILLUSTRATED BY JANET ROEMHILD.
Designed to enable anglers to establish immediately the kind of fish they have caught, this original, non-technical guide to fresh- and salt-water game fishes is also a handbook of game-fish facts. 153 fish illustrated: 81 in full color, 72 in black and white.

AUDUBON LAND BIRD GUIDE—RICHARD H. POUGH. ILLUSTRATED BY DON ECKELBERRY.
A distinguished ornithologist and an outstanding nature artist have combined to create for the layman the most complete and fully illustrated guide to the land birds of eastern and central North America ever published. Over 400 full-color illustrations of 275 species.

WILD FLOWER GUIDE—EDGAR T. WHERRY, PH.D. ILLUSTRATED BY TABEA HOFMANN.
Neatly blending text and illustrations, this technically accurate volume makes it easy to locate all information about any wild flower found in the northeastern and midland United States—its common name, scientific name, range, habitat, and suggestions as to how the plant can be cultivated. Over 500 species, 192 illustrated in full color and 236 in black and white.

THE INSECT GUIDE—RALPH B. SWAIN, PH.D. ILLUSTRATED BY SU ZAN N. SWAIN.
Lavishly illustrated and non-technical guide of the orders and major families of North American insects telling how to recognize, distinguish, find, capture, observe, preserve, and appreciate insects. 454 illustrations of 251 insect species: 330 in full color.

AUDUBON WATER BIRD GUIDE—RICHARD H. POUGH. ILLUSTRATED BY DON ECKLEBERRY & EARL L. POOLE.
This collaboration by an outstanding ornithologist and two exceptional artists is ideal for both home and field. There are 458 full-color and 138 black-and-white illustrations of 258 species.

MARINE GAME FISHES OF THE WORLD—FRANCESCA LA MONTE. ILLUSTRATED BY JANET ROEMHILD.
The first book of its kind ever to be written. Concisely summarized information about tackle, best angling methods, distribution, and habits of the fish at your bait as well as the names, seasonal grounds, and distinguishing characteristics of the fishes. 138 illustrations: 80 in full color; 58 in black and white.

THE MAMMAL GUIDE—RALPH S. PALMER. ILLUSTRATED BY THE AUTHOR.
No other book has ever presented as concisely and thoroughly so much information about the mammals of North America north of Mexico. 250 figures in full color of 182 species, 37 line drawings, 145 maps.

AUDUBON WESTERN BIRD GUIDE—RICHARD H. POUGH. ILLUSTRATED BY DON ECKELBERRY.
Ideal for use in both home and field, this complete and authoritative field guide includes 275 species indigenous to western North America including those species that stray from Asia. 478 illustrations: 340 in full color, 138 in black and white.

THE FERN GUIDE—EDGAR T. WHERRY, PH.D. ILLUSTRATED BY JAMES C. W. CHEN.
Botanists, naturalists, and amateur enthusiasts will relish this authoritative and concise guide to the northeastern and midland United States and adjacent Canada. 135 species of ferns selected and arranged for easy identification.